Introduction to Artificial Intelligence (AI)

Published 2024 by River Publishers

River Publishers

Alsbjergvej 10, 9260 Gistrup, Denmark

www.riverpublishers.com

Distributed exclusively by Routledge

605 Third Avenue, New York, NY 10017, USA

4 Park Square, Milton Park, Abingdon, Oxon OX14 4RN

Introduction to Artificial Intelligence (AI) / by Ahmed Banafa.

Routledge is an imprint of the Taylor & Francis Group, an informa business

ISBN 978-87-7004-186-7 (paperback)

ISBN 978-10-4009-479-2 (online)

ISBN 978-1-003-49952-7 (ebook master)

A Publication in the River Publishers Series in Rapids

While every effort is made to provide dependable information, the publisher, authors, and editors cannot be held responsible for any errors or omissions.

Introduction to Artificial Intelligence (AI)

Ahmed Banafa

San Jose State University, CA, USA

River Publishers

Routledge
Taylor & Francis Group

NEW YORK AND LONDON

Contents

Preface   vii

About the Author   ix

1 What is AI?   1

2 Neural Networks   9

3 Natural Language Processing (NLP)   15

4 Computer Vision   21

5 Levels of AI   27

6 Generative AI and Other Types of AI   31

7 Generative AI: Types, Skills, Opportunities and Challenges   37

8 Intellectual Abilities of Artificial Intelligence (AI)   45

9 Narrow AI vs. General AI vs. Super AI   51

Contents

10 Understanding The Psychological Impacts of Using AI   **55**

11 Ethics in AI   **61**

Index   **65**

Preface

Artificial intelligence (AI) has become one of the most transformative technologies of the 21st century, with the potential to revolutionize various industries and reshape our lives in ways we could have never imagined. From chatbots and virtual assistants to self-driving cars and medical diagnoses, AI has proven to be an invaluable tool in enhancing productivity, efficiency, and accuracy across different domains.

This book is an attempt to provide a comprehensive overview of the field of AI. It is designed to be an accessible resource for beginners, students, and professionals alike who are interested in understanding the concepts, applications, and implications of AI.

This book aims to provide a balanced perspective on AI, presenting its opportunities as well as its challenges. I hope that this book will serve as a useful resource for readers looking to learn more about this exciting and rapidly evolving field.

Readership:

Technical and nontechnical audience including: C-level executives, directors, lawyers, journalists, sales and marketing professionals, engineers, developers, and students.

Acknowledgement

I dedicate this book to my amazing wife for all her love and help.

About the Author

Professor Ahmed Banafa is a distinguished expert in IoT, blockchain, cybersecurity, and AI with a strong background in research, operations, and management. He has been recognized for his outstanding contributions, receiving the Certificate of Honor from the City and County of San Francisco, the Haskell Award for Distinguished Teaching from the University of Massachusetts Lowell, and the Author & Artist Award from San Jose State University. LinkedIn named him the No.1 tech voice to follow in 2018, acknowledging his predictive insights and influence. His groundbreaking research has been featured in renowned publications like Forbes, IEEE, and the MIT Technology Review. He has been interviewed by major media outlets including ABC, CBS, NBC, CNN, BBC, NPR, NHK, FOX, and The Washington Post. Being a member of the MIT Technology Review Global Panel further highlights his prominence in the tech community.

Prof. Banafa is an accomplished author known for impactful books. His work "Secure and Smart Internet of Things (IoT) using Blockchain and Artificial Intelligence (AI)" earned him the San Jose State University Author and Artist Award and recognition as one of the Best Technology Books of All Time and Best AI Models Books of All Time. His book on "Blockchain Technology and Applications" also received acclaim and is integrated into curricula at prestigious institutions like Stanford University. Additionally, he has contributed significantly to quantum computing through his third book, and he is preparing to release his fourth book on artificial intelligence in 2023. Prof. Banafa's educational journey includes cybersecurity studies at Harvard University and digital transformation studies at the Massachusetts Institute of Technology (MIT), culminating in a Master's Degree in Electrical Engineering and a Ph.D. in Artificial Intelligence.

1

What is AI?

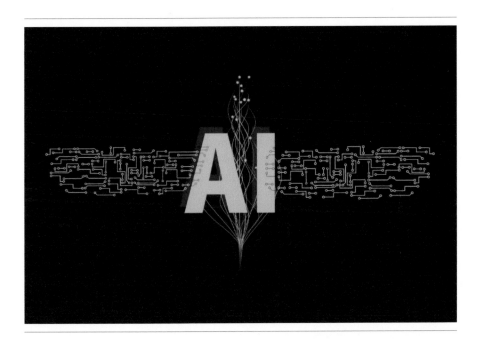

The field of artificial intelligence (AI) has a rich and fascinating history that stretches back over six decades. The story of AI is one of scientific inquiry, technological innovation, and the evolution of human thought about what it means to be intelligent. In this chapter, we will explore the major milestones in the history of AI and examine how this exciting field has evolved over time.

The origins of AI can be traced back to the 1950s, when researchers began to explore the possibility of creating machines that could think and reason like humans. One of the key figures in the early development of AI was the mathematician and logician Alan Turing. In his seminal paper "Computing Machinery and Intelligence," Turing proposed a test that would measure a machine's ability to exhibit intelligent behavior that was indistinguishable from that of a human. This test, known as the Turing Test, became a central concept in the study of AI.

In the years following Turing's work, researchers made significant progress in developing early AI systems. One of the earliest examples was the Logic Theorist, a program developed by Allen Newell and J.C. Shaw in 1955 that could prove mathematical theorems. Another landmark achievement was the creation of the General Problem Solver by Newell and Herbert Simon in 1957. This program was able to solve a range of problems by searching through a set of rules and making logical deductions.

The 1960s saw a surge of interest in AI, with researchers working to develop more advanced systems and applications. One notable example was the development of the first expert system, called Dendral, by Edward Feigenbaum and Joshua Lederberg in 1965. This system was designed to identify the molecular structure of organic compounds, and it proved to be highly successful in its field.

The 1970s and 1980s saw further advances in AI, with researchers developing new algorithms and techniques for machine learning, natural language processing, and computer vision. One of the key breakthroughs during this period was the development of the first neural network, which was inspired by the structure of the human brain. Another important development was the creation of rule-based expert systems, which allowed computers to make decisions based on a set of predefined rules.

In the 1990s and 2000s, AI continued to evolve rapidly, with researchers developing new techniques for deep learning, natural language processing, and image recognition. One of the most significant breakthroughs during this period was the development of the first autonomous vehicles, which used a combination of sensors, machine learning algorithms, and computer vision to navigate roads and highways.

Today, AI is a rapidly growing field that is transforming the way we live and work. From virtual assistants like Siri and Alexa to self-driving cars and sophisticated medical imaging systems, AI is playing an increasingly important role in our daily lives. Some of the most exciting developments in AI today include the development of advanced robots, the creation of AI-powered medical diagnosis tools, and the use of machine learning algorithms to analyze large amounts of data and identify patterns.

In conclusion, the history of AI is a story of scientific inquiry, technological innovation, and the evolution of human thought about what it means to be intelligent. From the early work of Turing and Newell to the breakthroughs of the present day, AI has come a long way in just a few short decades. As we look to the future, it is clear that AI will continue to play an increasingly important role in shaping the world around us, and we can only imagine what new breakthroughs and innovations lie ahead.

Artificial intelligence (AI) is a term that refers to the capability of machines or computer programs to perform tasks that typically require human intelligence, such as learning, problem-solving, and decision-making. The field of AI has been around for several decades, but recent advances in technology have led to a rapid increase in its capabilities and applications. In this chapter, we will explore what AI is, how it works, and its current and potential future applications.

AI can be broadly categorized into two types: narrow or weak AI and general or strong AI. Narrow AI is designed to perform specific tasks or solve specific problems, such as image recognition or language translation. It relies on machine learning algorithms that are trained on large datasets to recognize patterns and make predictions based on those patterns. General AI, on the other hand, aims to replicate human intelligence in a broad range of domains, such as reasoning, perception, and creativity. While narrow AI has made significant progress in recent years, general AI remains a long-term goal.

AI works by processing large amounts of data, identifying patterns and relationships, and using that information to make decisions or take actions. This process is made possible by algorithms that are designed to learn from the data they are fed. One of the most common types of AI algorithms is neural networks, which are modeled after the structure and function of the human brain. These networks consist of layers of interconnected nodes that process information and pass it on to the next layer, allowing the algorithm to identify patterns and relationships in the data.

AI has a wide range of applications across various industries and domains. In healthcare, for example, AI is being used to improve disease diagnosis and treatment by analyzing medical images and patient data. In finance, AI is being used to analyze market trends and make investment decisions. In transportation, AI is being used to optimize traffic flow and improve road safety. In education, AI is being used to personalize learning and improve student outcomes. These are just a few examples of the many ways in which AI is already being used to improve our lives.

Despite its many potential benefits, AI also raises several ethical and societal concerns. One of the biggest concerns is the potential impact of AI on employment. As AI becomes more advanced, it may be able to perform many tasks that are currently done by humans, leading to significant job losses. There are also concerns about the potential misuse of AI, such as the use of facial recognition technology for surveillance purposes. Additionally, there are concerns about the bias that may be built into AI algorithms, as they are only as unbiased as the data they are trained on.

Looking to the future, AI is likely to play an increasingly important role in our lives. As AI becomes more advanced, it will be able to perform more complex tasks and make more sophisticated decisions. This will have implications for virtually every aspect of society, from healthcare and finance to transportation and education. It will be important for policymakers and society as a whole to grapple with the ethical and societal implications of these developments and ensure that AI is used for the benefit of all.

In conclusion, AI is a rapidly advancing field that has the potential to revolutionize many aspects of our lives. It relies on algorithms that are designed to learn from data and identify patterns, and it has a wide range of applications across various industries and domains. While it raises many ethical and societal concerns, it also has the potential to bring significant benefits to society. As AI continues to advance, it will be important for society to grapple with these issues and ensure that its development is guided by ethical principles and used for the benefit of all.

What is Machine Learning?

Machine learning is a subset of artificial intelligence (AI) that involves the use of algorithms and statistical models to enable machines to learn from data and improve their performance on specific tasks. It is a rapidly growing field with numerous applications across various industries, including healthcare, finance, transportation, and more. In this chapter, we will explore what machine learning is, how it works, and its current and potential future applications.

At its core, machine learning involves the use of algorithms that enable machines to learn from data. These algorithms are designed to identify patterns and relationships in the data and use that information to make predictions or take actions. One of the most common types of machine learning algorithms is supervised learning, which involves training a model on a labeled dataset, where the correct output is known for each input. The model then uses this training data to make predictions on new, unseen data.

Another type of machine learning is unsupervised learning, which involves training a model on an unlabeled dataset and allowing it to identify patterns and relationships on its own. This type of learning is often used in applications such as clustering, where the goal is to group similar items together.

Reinforcement learning is another type of machine learning, which involves training a model to make decisions based on feedback from its environment. In this type of learning, the model learns through trial and error, adjusting its actions based on the rewards or punishments it receives.

Machine learning has numerous applications across various industries. In healthcare, for example, machine learning is being used to analyze medical images and patient data to improve disease diagnosis and treatment. In finance, machine learning is being used to analyze market trends and make investment decisions. In transportation, machine learning is being used to optimize traffic flow and improve road safety. In education, machine learning is being used to personalize learning and improve student outcomes. These are just a few examples of the many ways in which machine learning is being used to improve our lives.

One of the key advantages of machine learning is its ability to improve over time. As the machine is exposed to more data, it is able to improve its performance on specific tasks. This is known as "learning by experience." Machine learning models can also be used to make predictions or decisions in real-time, allowing them to be used in applications where speed is critical.

Despite its many benefits, machine learning also raises several ethical and societal concerns. One of the biggest concerns is the potential bias that may be built into machine learning algorithms. If the training data is biased, the model will also be biased, potentially leading to unfair decisions or outcomes. Another concern is the potential impact of machine learning on employment, as machines may be able to perform many tasks that are currently done by humans, leading to significant job losses.

Looking to the future, machine learning is likely to play an increasingly important role in our lives. As the amount of data being generated continues to increase, machine learning will be essential for making sense of this data and extracting valuable insights. It will also be important for society to grapple with the ethical and societal implications of these developments and ensure that machine learning is used for the benefit of all.

In conclusion, machine learning is a rapidly growing field that involves the use of algorithms and statistical models to enable machines to learn from data and improve their performance on specific tasks. It has numerous applications across various industries and has the potential to revolutionize many aspects of our lives. While it raises many ethical and societal concerns, it also has the potential to bring significant benefits to society. As machine learning continues to advance, it will be important for society to grapple with these issues and ensure that its development is guided by ethical principles and used for the benefit of all.

What is Deep Learning?

Deep learning is a subset of machine learning that involves the use of artificial neural networks to enable machines to learn from data and perform complex tasks. It is a rapidly growing field that has revolutionized many industries, including healthcare, finance, and transportation. In this chapter, we will explore what deep learning is, how it works, and its current and potential future applications.

At its core, deep learning involves the use of artificial neural networks to enable machines to learn from data. These networks are inspired by the structure of the human brain and are composed of layers of interconnected nodes that process information. Each node in the network performs a simple calculation based on its inputs and outputs a result, which is then passed on to the next layer of nodes.

The process of training a deep learning model involves feeding it a large dataset and adjusting the weights of the connections between the nodes to minimize the difference between the predicted output and the actual output. This process is known as backpropagation and involves iteratively adjusting the weights of the connections between the nodes until the model is able to accurately predict the output for a given input.

One of the key advantages of deep learning is its ability to perform complex tasks, such as image recognition, speech recognition, and natural language processing. For example, deep learning models can be trained to recognize faces in images, transcribe speech to text, and generate human-like responses to natural language queries.

Deep learning has numerous applications across various industries. In healthcare, for example, deep learning is being used to analyze medical images and identify potential diseases. In finance, deep learning is being used to analyze market trends and make investment decisions. In transportation, deep learning is being used to develop self-driving cars. These are just a few examples of the many ways in which deep learning is being used to improve our lives.

One of the key challenges of deep learning is the amount of data required to train the models. Deep learning models typically require large amounts of labeled data to accurately learn the underlying patterns and relationships in the data. This can be a challenge in industries such as healthcare, where labeled data may be scarce or difficult to obtain.

Another challenge is the complexity of deep learning models. Deep learning models can be difficult to interpret, and it can be challenging to understand why they make the predictions or decisions that they do. This can be a concern in applications where the decisions made by the model may have significant consequences.

Looking to the future, deep learning is likely to play an increasingly important role in our lives. As the amount of data being generated continues to increase, deep learning will be essential for making sense of this data and extracting valuable insights. It will also be important for society to grapple with the ethical and societal implications of these developments and ensure that deep learning is used for the benefit of all.

In conclusion, deep learning is a rapidly growing field that involves the use of artificial neural networks to enable machines to learn from data and perform complex tasks. It has numerous applications across various industries and has the potential to revolutionize many aspects of our lives. While it raises many ethical and societal concerns, it also has the potential to bring significant benefits to society. As deep learning continues to advance, it will be important for society to grapple with these issues and ensure that its development is guided by ethical principles and used for the benefit of all.

2

Neural Networks

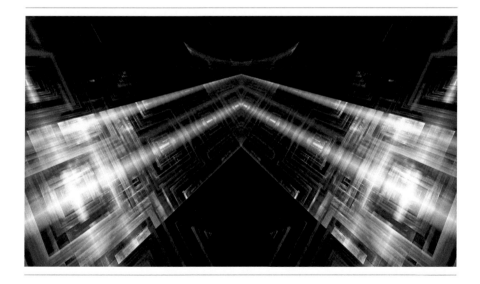

Neural networks are a type of artificial intelligence that have been inspired by the structure and function of the human brain. They are a computational model that is capable of learning from data and making predictions or decisions based on that learning. Neural networks are used in a variety of applications such as image recognition, speech recognition, natural language processing, and many more.

What is a Neural Network?

At its most basic level, a neural network is a collection of interconnected nodes, called neurons, which work together to process and analyze data. Each neuron in a neural network receives inputs from other neurons and produces an output that is transmitted to other neurons in the network. The inputs to each neuron are weighted, meaning that some inputs are more important than others in determining the output of the neuron.

Neurons in a neural network are organized into layers, with each layer having a specific function in processing the data. The input layer is where the data is initially introduced into the network. The output layer produces the final result of the network's processing. Between the input and output layers are one or more hidden layers, which perform the majority of the processing in the network.

Training a Neural Network

The ability of a neural network to learn from data is what makes it so powerful. In order to train a neural network, a set of training data is provided to the network, along with the desired outputs for that data. The network then adjusts the weights of the connections between neurons to minimize the difference between the predicted output and the desired output. This process is known as backpropagation.

The number of layers and the number of neurons in each layer are important factors in determining the accuracy and speed of a neural network. Too few neurons or layers may result in the network being unable to accurately represent the complexity of the data being processed. Too many neurons or layers may result in overfitting, where the network is too specialized to the training data and unable to generalize to new data.

Applications of Neural Networks

Neural networks have a wide range of applications in areas such as image recognition, speech recognition, natural language processing, and many more. In image recognition, for example, a neural network can be trained to identify specific features of an image, such as edges or shapes, and use that information to recognize objects in the image.

In speech recognition, a neural network can be trained to identify the individual phonemes that make up words and use that information to transcribe spoken words into text. In natural language processing, a neural network can be trained to understand the meaning of words and sentences and use that understanding to perform tasks such as language translation or sentiment analysis.

Neural networks are a powerful tool for artificial intelligence that are capable of learning from data and making predictions or decisions based on that learning. They are modeled after the structure and function of the human brain and have a wide range of applications in areas such as image recognition, speech recognition, and natural language processing. With continued research and development, neural networks have the potential to revolutionize the way we interact with technology and each other.

Types of Neural Networks

Neural networks are a subset of machine learning algorithms that are inspired by the structure and function of the human brain. They are capable of learning from data and making predictions or decisions based on that learning. There are several different types of neural networks, each with their own unique characteristics and applications (Figure 2.1).

1. **Feedforward Neural Networks**
   Feedforward neural networks are the most basic type of neural network. They consist of one or more layers of neurons that are connected in a feedforward manner, meaning that the output of each neuron is passed as input to the next layer of neurons. Feedforward neural networks are typically used for classification or regression tasks, where the output is a single value or class label.

2. **Convolutional Neural Networks**
   Convolutional neural networks (CNNs) are a type of neural network that is commonly used in image and video recognition tasks. They consist of several layers of neurons that are designed to process images or videos in a hierarchical manner. The first layer of a CNN is typically a convolutional layer, which applies a series of filters to the input image to extract features such as edges or textures. The output of the convolutional layer is then passed to one or more fully connected layers for further processing and classification.

3. **Recurrent Neural Networks**
   Recurrent neural networks (RNNs) are a type of neural network that is designed to handle sequential data, such as speech or text. They consist of a series of interconnected neurons, with each neuron in the network receiving inputs from both the previous neuron in the sequence and the current input. RNNs are capable of learning long-term dependencies in the input data, making them well-suited for tasks such as language translation or speech recognition.

Figure 2.1: Types of neural networks.

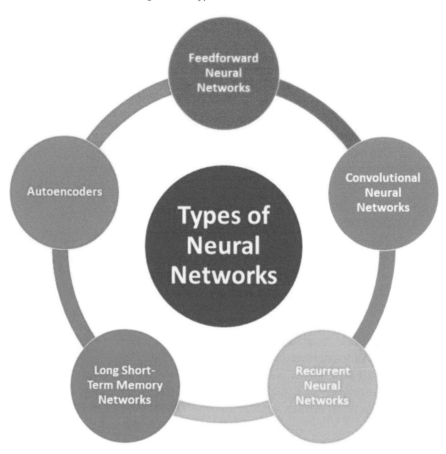

4. **Long Short-term Memory Networks**

   Long short-term memory (LSTM) networks are a type of RNN that is specifically designed to handle long-term dependencies in sequential data. They consist of a series of memory cells that can be selectively read, written to, or erased based on the input data. LSTMs are well-suited for tasks such as speech recognition or handwriting recognition, where the input data may have long-term dependencies that need to be captured.

5. **Autoencoders**

   Autoencoders are a type of neural network that is used for unsupervised learning tasks, such as feature extraction or data compression. They consist of an encoder network that takes the input data and maps it to a lower-dimensional latent space, and a decoder network that reconstructs the original input data from the latent space. Autoencoders are often used for tasks such as image or text generation, where the output is generated based on the learned features of the input data.

Neural networks are a powerful tool for machine learning that are capable of learning from data and making predictions or decisions based on that learning. There are several different types of neural networks, each with their own unique characteristics and applications. Feedforward neural networks are the most basic type of neural network, while convolutional neural networks are commonly used in image and video recognition tasks. Recurrent neural networks and long short-term memory networks are designed to handle sequential data, while autoencoders are used for unsupervised learning tasks such as feature extraction or data compression. With continued research and development, neural networks have the potential to revolutionize the way we interact with technology and each other.

3

Natural Language Processing (NLP)

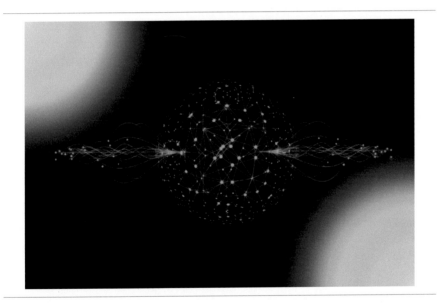

Natural language processing (NLP) is a subfield of artificial intelligence (AI) that focuses on the interaction between computers and humans using natural language. It involves analyzing, understanding, and generating human language in a way that is meaningful and useful to humans.

NLP has made significant strides in recent years, with the development of deep learning algorithms and the availability of large amounts of data. These advances have enabled NLP to be used in a wide range of applications, from language translation to chatbots to sentiment analysis.

In this article, we will explain the basics of NLP, its applications, and some of the challenges that researchers face.

The Basics of NLP

NLP involves several tasks, including:

1. Text classification: Assigning a category to a given text (e.g., spam or not spam).
2. Named entity recognition (NER): Identifying and classifying entities in a text, such as people, organizations, and locations.
3. Sentiment analysis: Determining the sentiment expressed in a text, whether it is positive, negative, or neutral.
4. Machine translation: Translating text from one language to another.
5. Question answering: Answering questions posed in natural language.
6. Text summarization: Generating a shorter summary of a longer text.

To accomplish these tasks, NLP algorithms use various techniques, such as:

1. Tokenization: Breaking a text into smaller units (tokens), such as words or subwords.
2. Part-of-speech (POS) tagging: Assigning a part of speech (e.g., noun, verb, adjective) to each token in a text.
3. Dependency parsing: Identifying the grammatical relationships between words in a sentence.
4. Named entity recognition: Identifying and classifying named entities in a text.
5. Sentiment analysis: Analyzing the tone of a text to determine whether it is positive, negative, or neutral.

Applications of NLP

NLP has numerous applications, including:

1. Chatbots: NLP can be used to build chatbots that can understand and respond to natural language queries.
2. Sentiment analysis: NLP can be used to analyze social media posts, customer reviews, and other texts to determine the sentiment expressed.
3. Machine translation: NLP can be used to translate text from one language to another, enabling communication across language barriers.
4. Voice assistants: NLP can be used to build voice assistants, such as Siri or Alexa, that can understand and respond to voice commands.
5. Text summarization: NLP can be used to generate summaries of longer texts, such as news articles or research papers.

Challenges in NLP

Despite the progress made in NLP, several challenges remain. Some of these challenges include:

1. Data bias: NLP algorithms can be biased if they are trained on data that is not representative of the population.
2. Ambiguity: Natural language can be ambiguous, and NLP algorithms must be able to disambiguate text based on context.
3. Out-of-vocabulary (OOV) words: NLP algorithms may struggle with words that are not in their training data.
4. Language complexity: Some languages, such as Chinese and Arabic, have complex grammatical structures that can make NLP more challenging.
5. Understanding context: NLP algorithms must be able to understand the context in which a text is written to correctly interpret its meaning.

NLP is a rapidly advancing field that has numerous applications, from chatbots to machine translation to sentiment analysis. As NLP continues to improve, we can expect to see more sophisticated language-based technologies emerge, such as virtual assistants that can understand and respond to complex queries. However, researchers must continue to address the challenges associated with NLP.

Natural Language Generation (NLG)

Natural language generation (NLG) is a subfield of natural language processing (NLP) that focuses on the automatic generation of human-like text. It involves transforming structured data into natural language that is understandable to humans. NLG has numerous applications, including automated report writing, chatbots, and personalized messaging.

In this chapter, we will explain the basics of NLG, its applications, and some of the challenges that researchers face.

The Basics of NLG

NLG involves several tasks, including:

1. Content determination: Deciding what information to include in the generated text.
2. Text structuring: Organizing the content into a coherent structure, such as paragraphs or bullet points.
3. Lexicalization: Selecting appropriate words and phrases to convey the intended meaning.

4. Referring expression generation: Determining how to refer to entities mentioned in the text, such as using pronouns or full names.
5. Sentence planning: Deciding how to structure individual sentences, such as choosing between active and passive voice.
6. Realization: Generating the final text.

To accomplish these tasks, NLG algorithms use various techniques, such as:

1. Template-based generation: Using pre-defined templates to generate text.
2. Rule-based generation: Applying rules to generate text.
3. Statistical-based generation: Using statistical models to generate text based on patterns in the data.
4. Neural-based generation: Using deep learning models to generate text.

Applications of NLG

NLG has numerous applications, including:

1. Automated report writing: NLG can be used to automatically generate reports, such as weather reports or financial reports, based on structured data.
2. Chatbots: NLG can be used to generate responses to user queries in natural language, enabling more human-like interactions with chatbots.
3. Personalized messaging: NLG can be used to generate personalized messages, such as marketing messages or product recommendations.
4. E-commerce: NLG can be used to automatically generate product descriptions based on structured data, improving the efficiency of e-commerce operations.
5. Content creation: NLG can be used to generate news articles or summaries based on structured data.

Challenges in NLG

Despite the progress made in NLG, several challenges remain. Some of these challenges include:

1. Data quality: NLG algorithms rely on high-quality structured data to generate accurate and useful text.
2. Naturalness: NLG algorithms must generate text that is natural-sounding and understandable to humans.
3. Domain specificity: NLG algorithms must be tailored to specific domains to generate accurate and useful text.
4. Personalization: NLG algorithms must be able to generate personalized text that is tailored to individual users.

5. Evaluation: Evaluating the quality of generated text is challenging, as it requires subjective judgments by humans.

NLG is a rapidly advancing field that has numerous applications, from automated report writing to chatbots to personalized messaging. As NLG continues to improve, we can expect to see more sophisticated and natural-sounding language-based technologies emerge, enabling more human-like interactions with machines. However, researchers must continue to address the challenges associated with NLG to ensure that generated text is accurate, natural-sounding, and useful.

4

Computer Vision

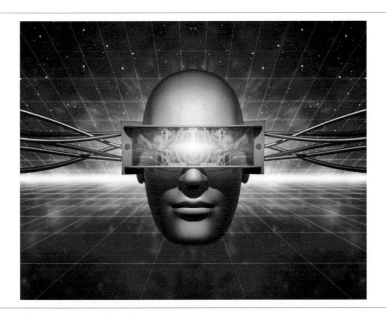

Computer vision is a field of study that enables computers to *interpret and understand* visual data from the world around us. This field has seen significant advancements in recent years, thanks to the increasing availability of *large datasets, powerful computing resources, and advanced algorithms.* In this chapter, we will explore the challenges and opportunities in the field of computer vision and its future.

What is Computer Vision?

Computer vision is a field of study that focuses on enabling computers to understand and interpret visual data from the world around us. It involves developing algorithms and techniques to enable computers to recognize, analyze, and process visual information from various sources such as images, videos, and depth maps.

The goal of computer vision is to enable machines *to see and understand the world in the same way humans do*. This requires the use of advanced algorithms and techniques that can extract useful information from visual data and use it to make decisions and take actions.

Applications of Computer Vision

Computer vision has a wide range of applications in various fields, some of which are listed below:

1. **Self-driving cars**: Computer vision is a key technology in the development of self-driving cars. It enables cars to detect and recognize objects such as pedestrians, other vehicles, and road signs, and make decisions based on that information.
2. **Facial recognition**: Computer vision is also used in facial recognition systems, which are used for security and surveillance purposes. It enables cameras to detect and recognize faces, and match them to a database of known individuals.
3. **Medical imaging**: Computer vision is used in medical imaging to analyze and interpret medical images such as X-rays, CT scans, and MRI scans. It enables doctors to detect and diagnose diseases and injuries more accurately and quickly.
4. **Industrial automation**: Computer vision is used in industrial automation to monitor and control manufacturing processes. It enables machines to detect and identify parts and products, and perform quality control checks.

Challenges in Computer Vision

Despite the significant progress in computer vision, there are still many challenges that need to be overcome. One of the biggest challenges is *developing algorithms and techniques that can work in real-world environments* with a high degree of variability and uncertainty. For example, recognizing objects in images and videos can be challenging when the lighting conditions, camera angle, and object orientation vary.

Another challenge *is developing algorithms that can process and analyze large volumes of visual data in real-time*. This is especially important in applications such as autonomous vehicles and robotics, where decisions need to be made quickly and accurately.

A third challenge *is developing algorithms that are robust to adversarial attacks.* Adversarial attacks are a type of attack where an attacker intentionally manipulates an image or video to deceive a computer vision system. For example, an attacker can add imperceptible noise to an image that can cause a computer vision system to misclassify an object.

Opportunities in Computer Vision

Despite the challenges, there are many opportunities in computer vision. One of the biggest opportunities is the *ability to automate tasks* that were previously performed by humans. For example, computer vision can be used to automate quality control in manufacturing, reduce errors in medical imaging, and improve safety in autonomous vehicles.

Another opportunity is *the ability to analyze large volumes of visual data* to gain insights and make predictions. For example, computer vision can be used to analyze satellite images to monitor crop health, detect changes in land use, and monitor environmental conditions.

A third opportunity *is the ability to develop new products and services* that can improve people's lives. For example, computer vision can be used to develop assistive technologies for the visually impaired, improve security and surveillance systems, and enhance virtual and augmented reality experiences.

Future of Computer Vision

The future of computer vision is very promising, and we can expect to see many new applications and advancements in this field. Some of the areas where we can expect to see significant progress include:

1. **Deep learning**: Deep learning is a subfield of machine learning that has shown remarkable progress in computer vision. We can expect to see continued advancements in deep learning algorithms, which will enable computers to recognize and interpret visual data more accurately and efficiently.
2. **Augmented and virtual reality**: Augmented and virtual reality are two areas where computer vision can have a significant impact. We can expect to see new applications and advancements in these areas that will enhance our experiences and improve our ability to interact with the world around us.

Figure 4.1: Future of computer vision and AI.

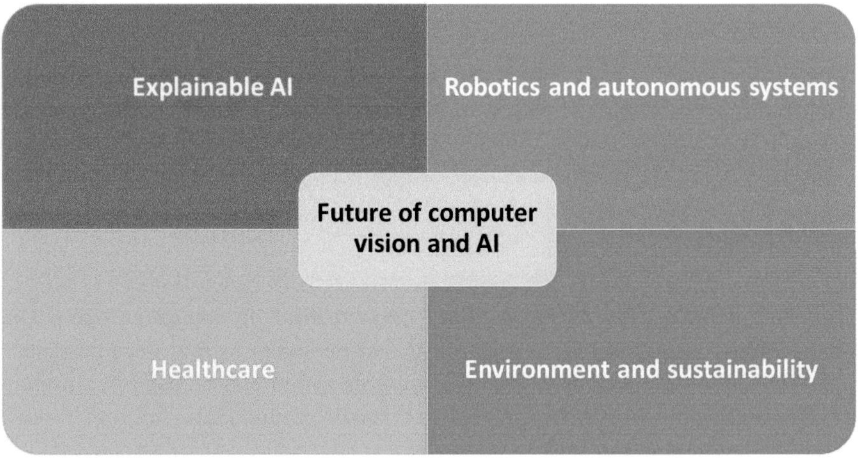

3. **Autonomous vehicles**: Autonomous vehicles are one of the most promising applications of computer vision. We can expect to see continued advancements in autonomous vehicle technology, which will enable safer and more efficient transportation.

Computer vision is a rapidly growing field that has many challenges and opportunities. Despite the challenges, we can expect to see many new applications and advancements in this field that will improve our ability to interpret and understand visual data from the world around us. As computer vision continues to evolve, we can expect to see new products and services that will improve people's lives and transform industries.

Future of Computer Vision and AI

The future of computer vision and AI is very promising, and we can expect to see many new applications and advancements in these fields. Some of the areas where we can expect to see significant progress include (Figure 4.1):

1. **Explainable AI**: Developing AI systems that can explain their reasoning and decision-making processes is critical for ensuring trust and transparency in AI systems. We can expect to see continued advancements in explainable AI, which will enable us to better understand and trust the decisions made by AI systems.
2. **Robotics and autonomous systems**: Robotics and autonomous systems are two areas where computer vision and AI can have a significant impact. We can expect to see continued

advancements in these areas that will enable us to develop more advanced and capable robots and autonomous systems.

3. **Healthcare:** Healthcare is an area where computer vision and AI can be used to improve patient outcomes and reduce costs. We can expect to see continued advancements in medical imaging and diagnostics, personalized medicine, and drug discovery, which will help to improve patient care and reduce healthcare costs.

4. **Environment and sustainability**: Computer vision and AI can be used to monitor and manage the environment, including monitoring pollution, tracking wildlife populations, and monitoring climate change. We can expect to see continued advancements in these areas that will help to improve our understanding of the environment and enable us to make better decisions about how to manage it.

Computer vision and AI are two rapidly growing fields that have many challenges and opportunities. Despite the challenges, we can expect to see many new applications and advancements in these fields that will improve our ability to understand and interpret data from the world around us. As computer vision and AI continue to evolve, we can expect to see new products and services that will improve people's lives and transform industries.

5

Levels of AI

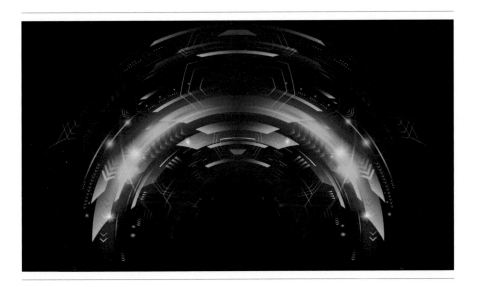

Artificial intelligence (AI) is one of the most rapidly advancing fields of technology today, with the potential to revolutionize virtually every industry and aspect of our daily lives. AI is often categorized into different levels based on their capabilities and autonomy, which can help us understand the current state of AI development and the challenges ahead (Figure 5.1).

Figure 5.1: AI levels.

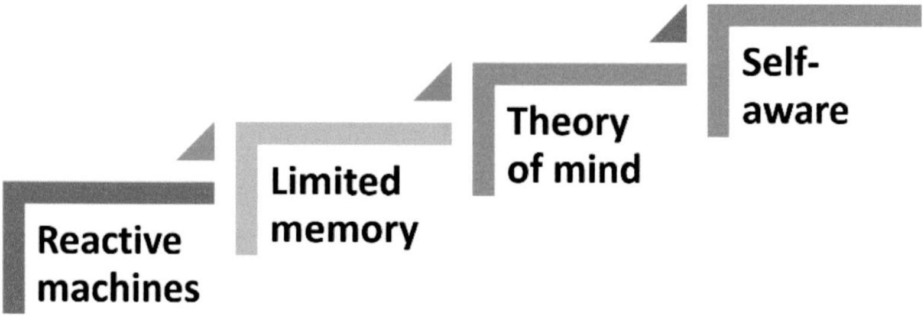

Level 1: Reactive machines.

The simplest form of AI is the reactive machine, which only reacts to inputs without any memory or ability to learn from experience. Reactive machines are programmed to perform specific tasks and are designed to respond to particular situations in pre-defined ways. They do not have any past data or memory to draw from, and they do not have the ability to consider the wider context of their actions.

One example of a reactive machine is IBM's Deep Blue, which defeated the chess champion Garry Kasparov in 1997. Deep Blue used an algorithm to evaluate millions of possible moves and choose the best one based on a set of pre-defined rules. Another example is the Roomba robotic vacuum cleaner, which senses its environment and navigates around it, but does not have the ability to remember its previous cleaning routes.

Level 2: Limited memory

. Limited memory AI can store past data and experiences to make informed decisions based on patterns and past experiences. This type of AI is commonly used in recommendation systems in e-commerce, where past purchases or browsing behavior is used to recommend future purchases.

Limited memory AI systems are designed to learn from experience and improve over time. For example, voice assistants such as Siri, Alexa, and Google Assistant use natural language processing and machine learning to understand and respond to user queries. These systems can also learn from past interactions with users, adapting to their preferences and improving their responses over time.

Level 3: Theory of mind

. Theory of mind AI goes beyond reactive and limited memory systems, simulating human-like thoughts and emotions and having a deeper understanding of human behavior and social interactions. This type of AI is still in the research phase and has not yet been fully developed.

Theory of mind AI has the potential to revolutionize fields such as psychology and social sciences, by providing insights into how humans think and interact with each other. One example of theory of mind AI is the work being done by the MIT Media Lab's Affective Computing Group, which is developing algorithms to recognize and respond to human emotions based on facial expressions, tone of voice, and other cues.

Level 4: Self-aware

. Self-aware AI is the most advanced level of AI, possessing the ability to not only understand human emotions and behaviors but also to be aware of their own existence and consciousness. This level of AI is still a theoretical concept and has not yet been achieved.

Self-aware AI has the potential to be truly transformative, with the ability to reflect on their own experiences and make autonomous decisions based on their own motivations and goals. However, the development of self-aware AI also raises important ethical and philosophical questions about the nature of consciousness, free will, and the relationship between humans and machines.

Conclusion

The levels of AI provide a useful framework for understanding the current state of AI development and the challenges ahead. While reactive and limited memory AI are already being used in many applications today, theory of mind and self-aware AI are still in the research phase and may take decades or even centuries to fully develop.

As AI continues to advance, it is important to consider the ethical, social, and philosophical implications of this technology. AI has the potential to transform our society and economy, but it also raises important questions about the nature of intelligence, consciousness, and human–machine interactions. By considering the levels of AI and their implications, we can better understand the opportunities and challenges ahead as we continue to push the boundaries of artificial intelligence.

6

Generative AI and Other Types of AI

AI refers to the development of computer systems that can perform tasks that typically require human intelligence, such as learning, reasoning, problem-solving, perception, and natural language understanding.

AI is based on the idea of creating intelligent machines that can work and learn like humans. These machines can be trained to recognize patterns, understand speech, interpret data, and make decisions based on that data. AI has many practical applications, including speech recognition, image recognition, natural language processing, autonomous vehicles, and robotics, to name a few.

Types of AI

Narrow AI, also known as weak AI, is an AI system designed to perform a specific task or set of tasks. These tasks are often well-defined and narrow in scope, such as image recognition, speech recognition, or language translation. Narrow AI systems rely on specific algorithms and techniques to solve problems and make decisions within their domain of expertise. These systems do not possess true intelligence, but rather mimic intelligent behavior within a specific domain.

General AI, also known as strong AI or human-level AI, is an AI system that can perform any intellectual task that a human can do. General AI would have the ability to reason, learn, and understand any intellectual task that a human can perform. It would be capable of solving problems in a variety of domains, and would be able to apply its knowledge to new and unfamiliar situations. General AI is often thought of as the ultimate goal of AI research, but is currently only a theoretical concept.

Super AI, also known as artificial superintelligence, is an AI system that surpasses human intelligence in all areas. Super AI would be capable of performing any intellectual task with ease, and would have an intelligence level far beyond that of any human being. Super AI is often portrayed in science fiction as a threat to humanity, as it could potentially have its own goals and motivations that could conflict with those of humans. Super AI is currently only a theoretical concept, and the development of such a system is seen as a long-term goal of AI research.

Technical Types of AI (Figure 6.1)

1. **Rule-based AI**: Rule-based AI, also known as expert systems, is a type of AI that relies on a set of pre-defined rules to make decisions or recommendations. These rules are typically created by human experts in a particular domain, and are encoded into a computer program. Rule-based AI is useful for tasks that require a lot of domain-specific knowledge, such as medical diagnosis or legal analysis.

2. **Supervised learning:** Supervised learning is a type of machine learning that involves training a model on a labeled dataset. This means that the dataset includes both input data and the correct output for each example. The model learns to map input data to output data, and can

Figure 6.1: Technical types of AI.

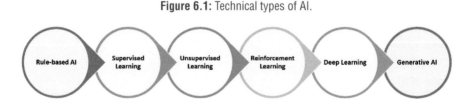

then make predictions on new, unseen data. Supervised learning is useful for tasks such as image recognition or natural language processing.

3. **Unsupervised learning:** Unsupervised learning is a type of machine learning that involves training a model on an unlabeled dataset. This means that the dataset only includes input data, and the model must find patterns or structure in the data on its own. Unsupervised learning is useful for tasks such as clustering or anomaly detection.

4. **Reinforcement learning:** Reinforcement learning is a type of machine learning that involves training a model to make decisions based on rewards and punishments. The model learns by receiving feedback in the form of rewards or punishments based on its actions, and adjusts its behavior to maximize its reward. Reinforcement learning is useful for tasks such as game playing or robotics.

5. **Deep learning:** Deep learning is a type of machine learning that involves training deep neural networks on large datasets. Deep neural networks are neural networks with multiple layers, allowing them to learn complex patterns and structures in the data. Deep learning is useful for tasks such as image recognition, speech recognition, and natural language processing.

6. **Generative AI**: Generative AI is a type of AI that is used to generate new content, such as images, videos, or text. It works by using a model that has been trained on a large dataset of examples, and then uses this knowledge to generate new content that is similar to the examples it has been trained on. Generative AI is useful for tasks such as computer graphics, natural language generation, and music composition.

Generative AI

Generative AI is a type of artificial intelligence that is used to generate new content, such as images, videos, or even text. It works by using a model that has been trained on a large dataset of examples, and then uses this knowledge to generate new content that is similar to the examples it has been trained on.

One of the most exciting applications of generative AI is in the field of computer graphics. By using generative models, it is possible to create realistic images and videos that look like they were captured in the real world. This can be incredibly useful for a wide range of applications, from creating realistic game environments to generating lifelike product images for e-commerce websites.

Another application of generative AI is in the field of natural language processing. By using generative models, it is possible to generate new text that is similar in style and tone to a particular author or genre. This can be useful for a wide range of applications, from generating news articles to creating marketing copy.

One of the key advantages of generative AI is its ability to create new content that is both creative and unique. Unlike traditional computer programs, which are limited to following a fixed set of rules, generative AI is able to learn from examples and generate new content that is similar, but not identical, to what it has seen before. This can be incredibly useful for applications where creativity and originality are important, such as in the arts or in marketing.

However, there are also some potential drawbacks to generative AI. One of the biggest challenges is ensuring that the content generated by these models is not biased or offensive. Because these models are trained on a dataset of examples, they may inadvertently learn biases or stereotypes that are present in the data. This can be especially problematic in applications like natural language processing, where biased language could have real-world consequences.

Another challenge is ensuring that the content generated by these models is of high quality. Because these models are based on statistical patterns in the data, they may occasionally produce outputs that are nonsensical or even offensive. This can be especially problematic in applications like chatbots or customer service systems, where errors or inappropriate responses could damage the reputation of the company or organization.

Despite these challenges, however, the potential benefits of generative AI are enormous. By using generative models, it is possible to create new content that is both creative and unique, while also being more efficient and cost-effective than traditional methods. With continued research and development, generative AI could play an increasingly important role in a wide range of applications, from entertainment and marketing to scientific research and engineering.

One of the challenges in creating effective generative AI models is choosing the right architecture and training approach. There are many different types of generative models, each with its own strengths and weaknesses. Some of the most common types of generative models include variational autoencoders, generative adversarial networks, and autoregressive models.

Variational autoencoders are a type of generative model that uses an encoder–decoder architecture to learn a compressed representation of the input data, which can then be used to generate new content. This approach is useful for applications where the input data is high-dimensional, such as images or video.

Generative adversarial networks (GANs) are another popular approach to generative AI. GANs use a pair of neural networks to generate new content. One network generates new content, while the other network tries to distinguish

Figure 6.2: Risks of generative AI.

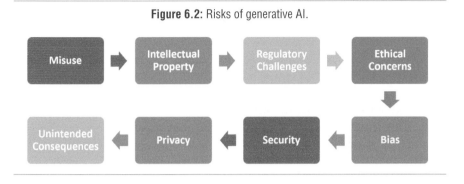

between real and fake content. By training these networks together, GANs are able to generate content that is both realistic and unique.

Autoregressive models are a type of generative model that uses a probabilistic model to generate new content. These models work by predicting the probability of each output.

Risks of Generative AI

Generative AI has the potential to revolutionize many industries and bring about numerous benefits, but it also poses several risks that need to be addressed. Here are some of the most significant risks associated with generative AI (Figure 6.2).

1. **Misuse**: Generative AI can be used to create fake content that is difficult to distinguish from real content, such as deepfakes. This can be used to spread false information or create misleading content that could have serious consequences.
2. **Bias**: Generative AI systems learn from data, and if the data is biased, then the system can also be biased. This can lead to unfair or discriminatory outcomes in areas such as hiring or lending.
3. **Security**: Generative AI can be used to create new forms of cyber attacks, such as creating realistic phishing emails or malware that can evade traditional security measures.
4. **Intellectual property**: Generative AI can be used to create new works that may infringe on the intellectual property of others, such as using existing images or music to generate new content.
5. **Privacy**: Generative AI can be used to create personal information about individuals, such as realistic images or videos that could be used for identity theft or blackmail.
6. **Unintended consequences**: Generative AI systems can create unexpected or unintended outcomes, such as creating new types of malware or causing harm to individuals or society.
7. **Regulatory challenges**: The use of generative AI raises regulatory challenges related to its development, deployment, and use, including questions around accountability and responsibility.

8. **Ethical concerns**: The use of generative AI raises ethical concerns, such as whether it is appropriate to create content that is indistinguishable from real content, or whether it is ethical to use generative AI for military or surveillance purposes.

Future of Generative AI

Generative AI is a rapidly advancing field that holds enormous potential for many different applications. As the technology continues to develop, we can expect to see some exciting advancements and trends in the future of generative AI. Here are some possible directions for the field:

Improved natural language processing (NLP): Natural language processing is one area where generative AI is already making a big impact, and we can expect to see this trend continue in the future. Advancements in NLP will allow for more natural-sounding and contextually appropriate responses from chatbots, virtual assistants, and other AI-powered communication tools.

Increased personalization: As generative AI systems become more sophisticated, they will be able to generate content that is more tailored to individual users. This could mean everything from personalized news articles to custom video game levels that are generated on the fly.

Enhanced creativity: Generative AI is already being used to generate music, art, and other forms of creative content. As the technology improves, we can expect to see more and more AI-generated works of art that are indistinguishable from those created by humans.

Better data synthesis: As data sets become increasingly complex, generative AI will become an even more valuable tool for synthesizing and generating new data. This could be especially important in scientific research, where AI-generated data could help researchers identify patterns and connections that might otherwise go unnoticed.

Increased collaboration: One of the most exciting possibilities for generative AI is its potential to enhance human creativity and collaboration. By providing new and unexpected insights, generative AI could help artists, scientists, and other creatives work together in novel ways to generate new ideas and solve complex problems.

The future of generative AI looks bright, with plenty of opportunities for innovation and growth in the years ahead.

7

Generative AI: Types, Skills, Opportunities and Challenges

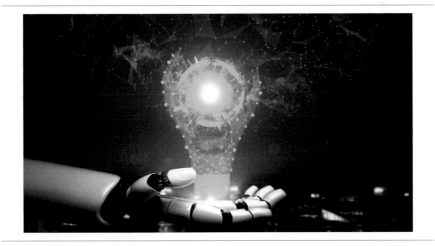

Generative AI refers to a class of machine learning techniques that aim to generate new data that is similar to, but not identical to, the data it was trained on. In other words, generative AI models learn to create new data samples that have similar statistical properties to the training data, allowing them to create new content such as images, videos, audio, or text that has never been seen before.

Figure 7.1: Types of generative AI models

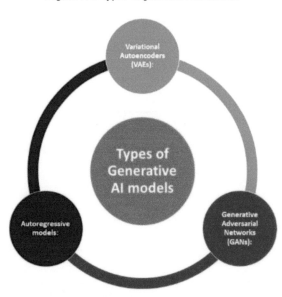

There are several types of generative AI models, including (Figure 7.1):

1. **Variational autoencoders (VAEs)**: A VAE is a type of generative model that learns to encode input data into a lower-dimensional latent space, then decode the latent space back into an output space to generate new data that is similar to the original input data. VAEs are commonly used for image and video generation.
2. **Generative adversarial networks (GANs):** A GAN is a type of generative model that learns to generate new data by pitting two neural networks against each other – a generator and a discriminator. The generator learns to create new data samples that can fool the discriminator, while the discriminator learns to distinguish between real and fake data samples. GANs are commonly used for image, video, and audio generation.
3. **Autoregressive models**: Autoregressive models are a type of generative model that learns to generate new data by predicting the probability distribution of the next data point given the previous data points. These models are commonly used for text generation.

Skills needed to work in generative AI:

1. **Strong mathematical and programming skills**: In generative AI, you'll be working with complex algorithms and models that require a solid understanding of mathematical concepts such as linear algebra, calculus, probability theory, and optimization algorithms. Additionally,

you'll need to be proficient in programming languages such as Python, TensorFlow, PyTorch, or Keras, which are commonly used in generative AI research and development.

2. **Deep learning expertise**: Generative AI involves the use of deep learning techniques and frameworks, which require a deep understanding of how they work. You should have experience with various deep learning models, such as convolutional neural networks (CNNs), recurrent neural networks (RNNs), and transformer-based models, as well as experience with training, fine-tuning, and evaluating these models.

3. **Understanding of natural language processing (NLP):** If you're interested in generative AI for NLP, you should have experience with NLP techniques such as language modeling, text classification, sentiment analysis, and machine translation. You should also be familiar with NLP-specific deep learning models, such as transformers and encoder-decoder models.

4. **Creative thinking**: In generative AI, you'll be tasked with generating new content, such as images, music, or text. This requires the ability to think creatively and come up with innovative ideas for generating content that is both novel and useful.

5. **Data analysis skills**: Generative AI requires working with large datasets, so you should have experience with data analysis and visualization techniques. You should also have experience with data preprocessing, feature engineering, and data augmentation to prepare data for training and testing models.

6. **Collaboration skills**: Working in generative AI often requires collaborating with other team members, such as data scientists, machine learning engineers, and designers. You should be comfortable working in a team environment and communicating technical concepts to non-technical stakeholders.

7. **Strong communication skills**: As a generative AI expert, you'll be communicating complex technical concepts to both technical and non-technical stakeholders. You should have strong written and verbal communication skills to effectively explain your work and findings to others.

8. **Continuous learning**: Generative AI is a rapidly evolving field, and staying up-to-date with the latest research and techniques is essential to stay competitive. You should have a strong appetite for continuous learning and be willing to attend conferences, read research papers, and experiment with new techniques to improve your skills.

Overall, working in generative AI requires a mix of technical, creative, and collaborative skills. By developing these skills, you'll be well-equipped to tackle challenging problems in this exciting and rapidly evolving field.

Generative AI opportunities (Figure 7.2):

1. **Creative content generation**: One of the most exciting opportunities in generative AI is the ability to create new and unique content in various domains such as art, music, literature, and design. Generative AI can help artists and designers to create new and unique pieces of work that may not have been possible otherwise.

2. **Improved personalization**: Generative AI can also help businesses to provide more personalized experiences to their customers. For example, it can be used to generate

Figure 7.2: Generative AI opportunities.

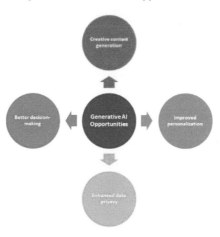

personalized recommendations, product designs, or content for users based on their preferences.

3. **Enhanced data privacy**: Generative AI can be used to generate synthetic data that mimics the statistical properties of real data, which can be used to protect users' privacy. This can be particularly useful in healthcare, where sensitive medical data needs to be protected.

4. **Better decision-making**: Generative AI can also be used to generate alternative scenarios to help decision-makers make better-informed decisions. For example, it can be used to simulate different scenarios in finance, weather forecasting, or traffic management.

Generative AI challenges (Figure 7.3):

1. **Data quality**: Generative AI models heavily rely on the quality and quantity of data used to train them. Poor-quality data can result in models that generate low-quality outputs, which can impact their usability and effectiveness.

2. **Ethical concerns**: Generative AI can raise ethical concerns around the use of synthesized data, particularly in areas such as healthcare, where synthetic data may not accurately reflect real-world data. Additionally, generative AI can be used to create fake media, which can have negative consequences if misused.

3. **Limited interpretability**: Generative AI models can be complex and difficult to interpret, making it hard to understand how they generate their outputs. This can make it difficult to diagnose and fix errors or biases in the models.

4. **Resource-intensive**: Generative AI models require significant computing power and time to train, making it challenging to scale them for large datasets or real-time applications.

Figure 7.3: Generative AI challenges.

5. **Fairness and bias**: Generative AI models can perpetuate biases present in the training data, resulting in outputs that are discriminatory or unfair to certain groups. Ensuring fairness and mitigating biases in generative AI models is an ongoing challenge.

Generative AI has numerous applications in various fields, including art, design, music, and literature. For example, generative AI models can be used to create new art, design new products, compose new music, or write new stories. Generative AI is also used in healthcare for generating synthetic medical data to protect patients' privacy, or in cybersecurity to generate fake data to test security systems.

ChatGPT

ChatGPT is a specific implementation of generative AI. Generative AI is a broad category of machine learning algorithms that are used to generate new data based on patterns learned from existing data. In the context of natural language processing, generative AI can be used to generate new text based on patterns learned from a large corpus of text data.

ChatGPT is a specific implementation of generative AI that is designed to generate text in response to user input in a conversational setting. ChatGPT is based on the GPT (generative pre-trained transformer) architecture, which is a type of neural network that has been pre-trained on a massive amount of text data. This pre-training allows ChatGPT to generate high-quality text that is both fluent and coherent.

In other words, ChatGPT is a specific application of generative AI that is designed for conversational interactions. Other applications of generative AI may include language translation, text summarization, or content generation for marketing purposes.

Overall, the relationship between generative AI and ChatGPT is that ChatGPT is an implementation of generative AI that is specifically designed for conversational interactions. As a result, ChatGPT is a powerful tool for natural language processing that can be used in a wide range of applications, from customer service to education to healthcare.

As an AI language model, ChatGPT's future is constantly evolving and growing. With a temperature of 0.9, ChatGPT has the potential to generate more imaginative and unexpected responses, albeit at the cost of potentially introducing errors and inconsistencies.

In the future, ChatGPT will likely continue to improve its natural language processing capabilities, allowing it to understand and respond to increasingly complex and nuanced queries. It may also become more personalized, utilizing data from users' interactions to tailor responses to individual preferences and needs.

Additionally, ChatGPT may be used in a wide range of industries and applications, such as customer service, education, and healthcare, providing users with instant access to information and support.

However, as with any emerging technology, ChatGPT will face challenges, such as ethical concerns surrounding its use, potential biases in its responses, and the need to ensure user privacy and security.

Overall, the future of ChatGPT is exciting and full of potential. With continued development and improvement, ChatGPT has the potential to revolutionize the way we interact with technology and each other, making communication faster, more efficient, and more personalized.

As an AI language model, ChatGPT has the potential to be used in a wide range of applications and industries. Here are some potential areas where ChatGPT could be used in the future:

1. **Customer service:** ChatGPT could be used by companies to provide instant and personalized support to their customers. Chatbots powered by ChatGPT could answer frequently asked questions, troubleshoot technical issues, and provide personalized recommendations to users.

2. **Education:** ChatGPT could be used in online learning environments to provide instant feedback and support to students. Chatbots powered by ChatGPT could answer students' questions, provide personalized feedback on assignments, and help students navigate complex topics.

3. **Healthcare:** ChatGPT could be used in telemedicine applications to provide patients with instant access to medical advice and support. Chatbots powered by ChatGPT could answer patients' questions, provide guidance on medication regimens, and help patients track their symptoms.

4. **Journalism:** ChatGPT could be used in newsrooms to help journalists quickly gather and analyze information on breaking news stories. Chatbots powered by ChatGPT could scan social media and other sources for relevant information, summarize key points, and help journalists identify potential angles for their stories.

5. **Personalized marketing:** ChatGPT could be used by marketers to provide personalized recommendations and support to customers. Chatbots powered by ChatGPT could analyze users' browsing history, purchase history, and other data to provide personalized product recommendations and marketing messages.

Of course, as with any emerging technology, ChatGPT will face challenges and limitations. Some potential issues include:

1. **Ethical concerns:** There are ethical concerns surrounding the use of AI language models like ChatGPT, particularly with regards to issues like privacy, bias, and the potential for misuse.

2. **Accuracy and reliability:** ChatGPT is only as good as the data it is trained on, and it may not always provide accurate or reliable information. Ensuring that ChatGPT is trained on high-quality data and that its responses are validated and verified will be crucial to its success.

3. **User experience:** Ensuring that users have a positive and seamless experience interacting with ChatGPT will be crucial to its adoption and success. This may require improvements in natural language processing and user interface design.

Overall, the future of ChatGPT is full of potential and promise. With continued development and improvement, ChatGPT has the potential to transform the way we interact with technology and each other, making communication faster, more efficient, and more personalized than ever before.

8

Intellectual Abilities of Artificial Intelligence (AI)

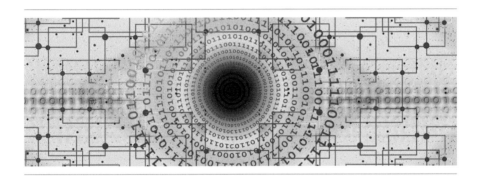

To understand AI's capabilities and abilities we need to recognize the different components and subsets of AI. Terms like neural networks, machine learning (ML), and deep learning need to be defined and explained.

In general, artificial intelligence (AI) refers to the simulation of human intelligence in machines that are programmed to think like humans and mimic their actions. The term may also be applied to any machine that exhibits traits associated with a human mind such as learning and problem-solving.

Neural Networks

In information technology, a neural network is a system of programs and data structures that approximates the operation of the human brain. A neural network usually involves a large number of processors operating in parallel,

Figure 8.1: Deep learning vs. machine learning.

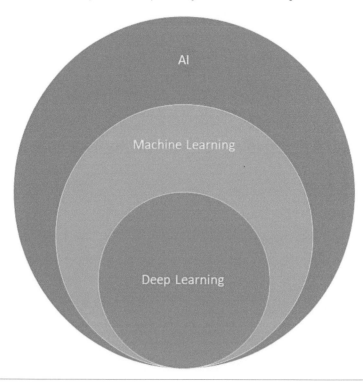

each with its own small sphere of knowledge and access to data in its local memory.

Typically, a neural network is initially "trained" or fed large amounts of data and rules about data relationships (for example, "A grandfather is older than a person's father"). A program can then tell the network how to behave in response to an external stimulus (for example, to input from a computer user who is interacting with the network) or can initiate activity on its own (within the limits of its access to the external world).

Deep Learning vs. Machine Learning (Figure 8.1)

To understand what deep learning is, it's first important to distinguish it from other disciplines within the field of AI.

One outgrowth of AI was machine learning, in which the computer extracts knowledge through supervised experience. This typically involved a human operator helping the machine learn by giving it hundreds or thousands of training examples, and manually correcting its mistakes.

While machine learning has become dominant within the field of AI, it does have its problems. For one thing, it's massively time consuming. For another, it's still not a true measure of machine intelligence since it relies on human ingenuity to come up with the abstractions that allow a computer to learn.

Unlike machine learning, deep learning is mostly *unsupervised*. It involves, for example, creating large-scale neural nets that allow the computer to learn and "think" by itself – without the need for direct human intervention.

Deep learning "really doesn't look like a computer program" where ordinary computer code is written in very strict logical steps, but what you'll see in deep learning is something different; you don't have a lot of instructions that say: "If one thing is true do this other thing".

Instead of linear logic, deep learning is based on theories of how the human brain works. The program is made of tangled layers of interconnected nodes. It learns by rearranging connections between nodes after each new experience.

Deep learning has shown potential as the basis for software that could work out the emotions or events described in text (even if they aren't explicitly referenced), recognize objects in photos, and make sophisticated predictions about people's likely future behavior. Example of deep learning in action is voice recognition like Google Now and Apple's Siri.

Deep learning is showing a great deal of promise –it will make self-driving cars and robotic butlers a real possibility. The ability to analyze massive data sets and use deep learning in computer systems that can adapt to experience, rather than depending on a human programmer, will lead to breakthroughs. These range from drug discovery to the development of new materials to robots with a greater awareness of the world around them.

Deep Learning and Affective Computing

Affective computing is the study and development of systems and devices that can recognize, interpret, process, and simulate human affects. It is an interdisciplinary field spanning computer science (deep learning), psychology, and cognitive science. While the origins of the field may be traced as far back as to early philosophical inquiries into emotion ("affect" is, basically, a synonym for "emotion."), the more modern branch of computer science originated with *Rosalind Picard's* 1995 paper on affective computing. A motivation for the research is the ability to simulate *empathy*. The machine should interpret the emotional state of humans and adapt its behavior to them, giving an appropriate response for those emotions.

Affective computing technologies using deep learning sense the emotional state of a user (via sensors, microphone, cameras and/or software logic) and respond by performing specific, predefined product/service features, such as changing a quiz or recommending a set of videos to fit the mood of the learner.

The more computers we have in our lives the more we're going to want them to behave politely, and be socially smart. We don't want it to bother us with unimportant information. That kind of common-sense reasoning requires an understanding of the person's *emotional state.*

One way to look at affective computing is *human–computer interaction* in which a device has the ability to detect and appropriately respond to its user's emotions and other stimuli. A computing device with this capacity could gather cues to user emotion from a variety of sources. Facial expressions, posture, gestures, speech, the force or rhythm of key strokes and the temperature changes of the hand on a mouse can all signify changes in the user's emotional state, and these can all be detected and interpreted by a computer. A built-in camera captures images of the user and algorithms are used to process the data to yield meaningful information. Speech recognition and gesture recognition are among the other technologies being explored for affective computing applications.

Recognizing emotional information requires the extraction of meaningful patterns from the gathered data. This is done using deep learning techniques that process different modalities, such as speech recognition, natural language processing, or facial expression detection.

Emotion in Machines

A major area in affective computing is the design of computational devices proposed to exhibit either innate emotional capabilities or that are capable of convincingly simulating emotions. A more practical approach, based on current technological capabilities, is the simulation of emotions in conversational agents in order to enrich and facilitate interactivity between human and machine. While human emotions are often associated with surges in hormones and other neuropeptides, emotions in machines might be associated with abstract states associated with progress (or lack of progress) in autonomous learning systems in this view, affective emotional states correspond to time-derivatives in the learning curve of an arbitrary learning system.

There are two major categories describing emotions in machines: *Emotional speech* and *facial affect detection.*

Emotional speech includes:

- Deep learning
- Databases
- Speech descriptors.

Facial affect detection includes:

- Body gesture
- Physiological monitoring.

The Future

Affective computing using deep learning tries to address one of the major drawbacks of online learning versus in-classroom learning: the teacher's capability to immediately adapt the pedagogical situation to the emotional state of the student in the classroom. In e-learning applications, affective computing using deep learning can be used to adjust the presentation style of a computerized tutor when a learner is bored, interested, frustrated, or pleased. Psychological health services, i.e. counseling, benefit from affective computing applications when determining a client's emotional state.

Robotic systems capable of processing affective information exhibit higher flexibility while one works in uncertain or complex environments. Companion devices, such as digital pets, use affective computing with deep learning abilities to enhance realism and provide a higher degree of autonomy.

Other potential applications are centered around social monitoring. For example, a car can monitor the emotion of all occupants and engage in additional safety measures, such as alerting other vehicles if it detects the driver as being angry. Affective computing with deep learning at the core has potential applications in human–computer interaction, such as affective mirrors allowing the user to see how he or she performs; emotion monitoring agents sending a warning before one sends an angry email; or even music players selecting tracks based on mood. Companies would then be able to use affective computing to infer whether their products will or will not be well received by the respective market. There are endless applications for affective computing with deep learning in all aspects of life.

9

Narrow AI vs. General AI vs. Super AI

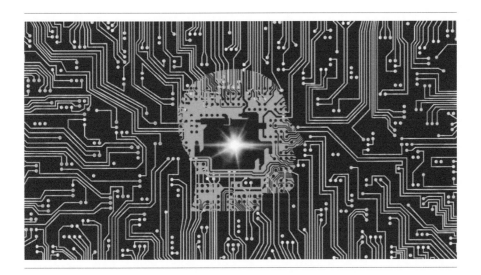

Artificial intelligence (AI) is a term used to describe machines that can perform tasks that normally require human intelligence, such as visual perception, speech recognition, decision-making, and language translation. AI is classified into three main types: narrow AI, general AI, and super AI. Each type of AI has its unique characteristics, capabilities, and limitations. In this chapter, we will explain the differences between these three types of AI.

Narrow AI

Narrow AI, also known as weak AI, refers to AI that is designed to perform a specific task or a limited range of tasks. It is the most common type of AI and is widely used in various applications such as facial recognition, speech recognition, image recognition, natural language processing, and recommendation systems.

Narrow AI works by using machine learning algorithms, which are trained on a large amount of data to identify patterns and make predictions. These algorithms are designed to perform specific tasks, such as identifying objects in images or translating languages. Narrow AI is not capable of generalizing beyond the tasks for which it is programmed, meaning that it cannot perform tasks that it has not been specifically trained to do.

One of the key advantages of narrow AI is its ability to perform tasks faster and more accurately than humans. For example, facial recognition systems can scan thousands of faces in seconds and accurately identify individuals. Similarly, speech recognition systems can transcribe spoken words with high accuracy, making it easier for people to interact with computers.

However, narrow AI has some limitations. It is not capable of reasoning or understanding the context of the tasks it performs. For example, a language translation system can translate words and phrases accurately, but it cannot understand the meaning behind the words or the cultural nuances that may affect the translation. Similarly, image recognition systems can identify objects in images, but they cannot understand the context of the images or the emotions conveyed by the people in the images.

General AI

General AI, also known as strong AI, refers to AI that is designed to perform any intellectual task that a human can do. It is a theoretical form of AI that is not yet possible to achieve. General AI would be able to reason, learn, and understand complex concepts, just like humans.

The goal of general AI is to create a machine that can think and learn in the same way that humans do. It would be capable of understanding language, solving problems, making decisions, and even exhibiting emotions. General AI would be able to perform any intellectual task that a human can do, including tasks that it has not been specifically trained to do.

One of the key advantages of general AI is that it would be able to perform any task that a human can do, including tasks that require creativity, empathy, and intuition. This would open up new possibilities for AI applications in fields such as healthcare, education, and the arts.

However, general AI also raises some concerns. The development of general AI could have significant ethical implications, as it could potentially surpass human intelligence and become a threat to humanity. It could also lead to widespread unemployment, as machines would be able to perform tasks that were previously done by humans. Here are a few examples of general AI:

1. **AlphaGo:** A computer program developed by Google's DeepMind that is capable of playing the board game Go at a professional level.
2. **Siri:** An AI-powered personal assistant developed by Apple that can answer questions, make recommendations, and perform tasks such as setting reminders and sending messages.
3. **ChatGPT:** a natural language processing tool driven by AI technology that allows you to have human-like conversations and much more with a chatbot. The language model can answer questions, and assist you with tasks such as composing emails, essays, and code.

Super AI

Super AI refers to AI that is capable of surpassing human intelligence in all areas. It is a hypothetical form of AI that is not yet possible to achieve. Super AI would be capable of solving complex problems that are beyond human capabilities and would be able to learn and adapt at a rate that far exceeds human intelligence.

The development of super AI is the ultimate goal of AI research. It would have the ability to perform any task that a human can do, and more. It could potentially solve some of the world's most pressing problems, such as climate change, disease, and poverty.

Possible examples from movies: Skynet (Terminator), Viki (iRobot), and Jarvis (Ironman).

Challenges and Ethical Implications of General AI and Super AI

The development of general AI and super AI poses significant challenges and ethical implications for society. Some of these challenges and implications are discussed below (Figure 9.1):

1. **Control and safety**: General AI and super AI have the potential to become more intelligent than humans, and their actions could be difficult to predict or control. It is essential to ensure that these machines are safe and do not pose a threat to humans. There is a risk that these machines could malfunction or be hacked, leading to catastrophic consequences.

Figure 9.1: Challenges and ethical implications of general AI and super AI.

Challenges and Ethical Implications of
General AI and Super AI

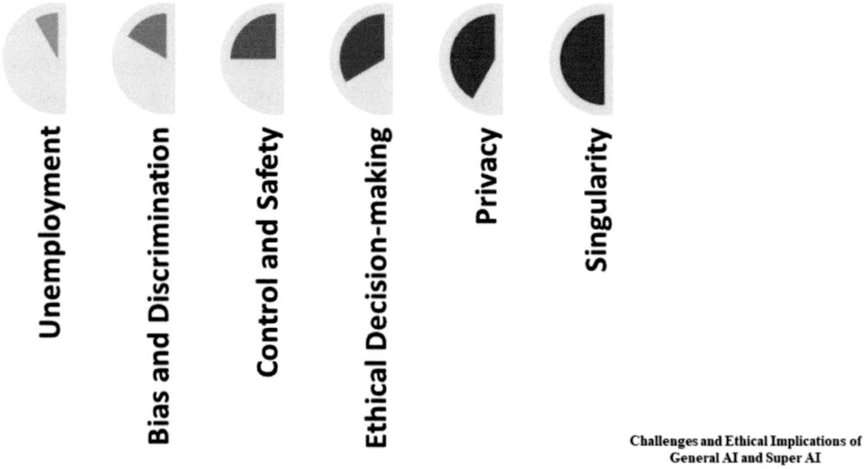

2. **Bias and discrimination**: AI systems are only as good as the data they are trained on. If the data is biased, the AI system will be biased as well. This could lead to discrimination against certain groups of people, such as women or minorities. There is a need to ensure that AI systems are trained on unbiased and diverse data.

3. **Unemployment**: General AI and super AI have the potential to replace humans in many jobs, leading to widespread unemployment. It is essential to ensure that new job opportunities are created to offset the job losses caused by these machines.

4. **Ethical decision-making**: AI systems are not capable of ethical decision-making. There is a need to ensure that these machines are programmed to make ethical decisions, and that they are held accountable for their actions.

5. **Privacy**: AI systems require vast amounts of data to function effectively. This data may include personal information, such as health records and financial data. There is a need to ensure that this data is protected and that the privacy of individuals is respected.

6. **Singularity**: Some experts have raised concerns that general AI or super AI could become so intelligent that they surpass human intelligence, leading to a singularity event. This could result in machines taking over the world and creating a dystopian future.

Narrow AI, general AI, and super AI are three different types of AI with unique characteristics, capabilities, and limitations. While narrow AI is already in use in various applications, general AI and super AI are still theoretical and pose significant challenges and ethical implications. It is essential to ensure that AI systems are developed ethically and that they are designed to benefit society as a whole

10

Understanding The Psychological Impacts of Using AI

Artificial intelligence (AI) has rapidly become integrated into many aspects of our daily lives, from personal assistants on our smartphones to the algorithms that underpin social media feeds. While AI has the potential to revolutionize the way we live and work, it is not without its drawbacks. One area of concern is the potential *psychological impacts of using AI systems*. As we become increasingly reliant on these technologies, there is growing concern that they may be having negative effects on our mental health and well-being. In this chapter, we will explore the potential psychological impacts of using AI systems and discuss strategies for minimizing these risks.

Figure 10.1: The potential psychological impacts of using AI.

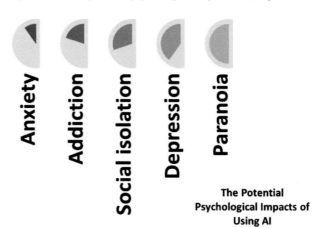

The Potential
Psychological Impacts of
Using AI

The potential psychological impacts of using AI (Figure 10.1):

- **Anxiety**: Some people may feel anxious when using AI systems because they are not sure how the system works or what outcomes to expect. For example, if someone is using a speech recognition system to transcribe their voice, they may feel anxious if they are unsure if the system is accurately capturing their words.
- **Addiction**: Overuse of technology, including AI systems, can lead to addictive behaviors. People may feel compelled to constantly check their devices or use AI-powered apps, which can interfere with other aspects of their lives, such as work or social relationships.
- **Social isolation**: People who spend too much time interacting with AI systems may become socially isolated, as they may spend less time engaging with other people in person. This can lead to a reduced sense of community or connection to others.
- **Depression**: Some people may experience depression or a sense of helplessness when interacting with AI systems that they perceive as being superior or more capable than they are. For example, if someone is using an AI-powered personal assistant, they may feel inadequate or helpless if the system is better at completing tasks than they are.
- **Paranoia**: Concerns around the safety and security of AI systems, as well as fears of AI taking over or replacing human decision-making, can lead to paranoid thinking in some individuals. This is particularly true in cases where AI systems are used to control physical systems, such as autonomous vehicles or weapons systems.

It's important to note that *not everyone* will experience these negative psychological impacts when using AI systems, and many people find AI to be helpful and beneficial. However, it's important to be aware of the potential risks associated with technology use and to take steps to mitigate these risks when possible.

There are several steps you can take to minimize the potential negative psychological impacts of using AI systems:

- **Set boundaries**: Establish clear boundaries for your use of AI systems, and try to limit your exposure to them. This can help prevent addiction and reduce feelings of anxiety or depression.
- **Stay informed**: Keep up-to-date with the latest developments in AI technology and try to understand how AI systems work. This can help reduce feelings of helplessness or paranoia and increase your confidence in using these systems.
- **Seek support**: If you are feeling anxious or stressed when using AI systems, talk to a trusted friend, family member, or mental health professional. They can provide support and help you work through your feelings.
- **Use AI systems responsibly**: When using AI systems, be mindful of their limitations and potential biases. Avoid relying solely on AI-generated information and always seek out multiple sources when making important decisions.
- **Take breaks**: Make sure to take regular breaks from using AI systems and spend time engaging in activities that promote relaxation and social connection. This can help reduce feelings of isolation and prevent addiction.
- **Advocate for ethical use of AI**: Support efforts to ensure that AI systems are developed and deployed in an ethical manner, with appropriate safeguards in place to protect privacy, autonomy, and other important values.

By following these steps, you can help ensure that your use of AI systems is positive and does not have negative psychological impacts.

Examples of incidents of psychological impacts of using AI:

- **AI-generated deepfake videos**: Deepfakes are videos that use AI to manipulate or replace an individual's image or voice in a video or audio recording. These videos can be used to spread false information or malicious content, which can have a severe psychological impact on the person depicted in the video.
- **Social media algorithms**: Social media platforms use AI algorithms to personalize the user experience by showing users content they are likely to engage with. However, this can create echo chambers where users only see content that aligns with their views, leading to confirmation bias and potentially increasing political polarization.
- **Job automation**: AI-powered automation can lead to job loss or significant changes in job roles and responsibilities. This can create anxiety and stress for employees who fear losing their jobs or having to learn new skills.
- **Bias in AI algorithms**: AI algorithms can perpetuate bias and discrimination, particularly in areas like criminal justice or hiring. This can harm marginalized groups and lead to feelings of injustice and discrimination.

- **Dependence on AI**: As people become increasingly reliant on AI-powered tools and devices, they may experience anxiety or stress when they cannot access or use these tools.
- **Surveillance and privacy concerns**: AI-powered surveillance tools, such as facial recognition technology, can infringe on privacy rights and create a sense of unease or paranoia in individuals who feel like they are being constantly monitored.
- **Mental health chatbots**: AI-powered chatbots have been developed to provide mental health support and guidance to individuals. While these tools can be helpful for some people, they can also lead to feelings of isolation and disconnection if users feel like they are not receiving personalized or empathetic support.
- **Addiction to technology**: With the increasing prevalence of AI-powered devices, people may become addicted to technology, leading to symptoms such as anxiety, depression, and sleep disorders.
- **Virtual assistants**: Virtual assistants, such as Siri or Alexa, can create a sense of dependency and make it harder for individuals to engage in real-life social interactions.
- **Gaming and virtual reality**: AI-powered gaming and virtual reality experiences can create a sense of immersion and escapism, potentially leading to addiction and detachment from real-life experiences.

The *responsibility* for the psychological impacts of using AI falls on various individuals and organizations, including (Figure 10.2):

Figure 10.2: The responsibility for the psychological impacts of using AI.

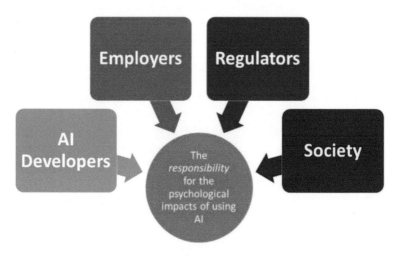

- **AI developers**: The developers of AI systems are responsible for ensuring that their systems are designed and programmed in a way that minimizes any negative psychological impacts on users. This includes considering factors such as transparency, privacy, and trustworthiness.
- **Employers**: Employers who use AI in the workplace have a responsibility to ensure that their employees are not negatively impacted by the use of AI. This includes providing training and support to help employees adjust to working with AI, as well as monitoring for any negative psychological impacts.
- **Regulators**: Government agencies and other regulatory bodies have a responsibility to ensure that the use of AI does not have negative psychological impacts on individuals. This includes setting standards and regulations for the design, development, and use of AI systems.
- **Society as a whole**: Finally, society as a whole has a responsibility to consider the psychological impacts of AI and to advocate for the development and use of AI systems that are designed with the well-being of individuals in mind. This includes engaging in public dialogue and debate about the appropriate use of AI, as well as advocating for policies that protect the rights and well-being of individuals impacted by AI.

Overall, the psychological impacts of AI are complex and multifaceted, and more research is needed to fully understand their effects.

11

Ethics in AI

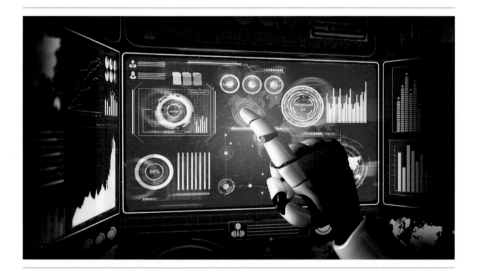

Artificial intelligence (AI) is transforming our world in countless ways, from healthcare to education, business to cybersecurity. While the potential benefits of AI are vast, there are also significant ethical considerations that must be taken into account. As intelligent machines become more prevalent in our society, it is crucial to consider the ethical implications of their use. In this chapter, I will explore some of the key ethical considerations in AI, including *bias, privacy, accountability, and transparency* (Figure 11.1).

Figure 11.1: Ethics in AI.

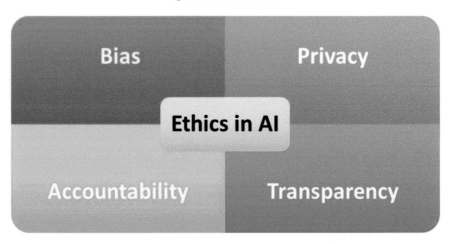

Bias in AI

One of the most significant ethical considerations in AI is *bias*. Bias can occur in AI systems when the data used to train them is biased or when the algorithms used to make decisions are biased. For example, facial recognition systems have been shown to be less accurate in identifying people with darker skin tones. This is because the data used to train these systems was primarily made up of images of lighter-skinned individuals. As a result, the system is more likely to misidentify someone with darker skin.

Bias in AI can have serious consequences, particularly in areas like healthcare and criminal justice. For example, if an AI system is biased against certain groups of people, it could lead to inaccurate diagnoses or unequal treatment. To address this issue, it is essential to ensure that the data used to train AI systems is diverse and representative of the entire population. Additionally, AI systems should be regularly audited to detect and correct any biases that may arise.

Privacy in AI

Another ethical consideration in AI is *privacy*. As AI systems become more prevalent, they are collecting and processing vast amounts of data about individuals. This data can include everything from personal information like names and addresses to sensitive information like medical records and financial information. It is essential to ensure that this data is protected and used only for its intended purpose.

One of the biggest risks to privacy in AI is the potential for data breaches. If an AI system is hacked or otherwise compromised, it could lead to the exposure of sensitive information. To mitigate this risk, it is crucial to ensure that AI systems are designed with security in mind. Additionally, individuals should be given control over their data and should be able to choose whether or not it is collected and used by AI systems.

Accountability in AI

As AI systems become more autonomous, it is crucial to consider the issue of *accountability*. If an AI system makes a mistake or causes harm, who is responsible? The answer to this question is not always clear, particularly in cases where AI systems are making decisions that have significant consequences. For example, if an autonomous vehicle causes an accident, who is responsible? The manufacturer of the vehicle? The owner of the vehicle? The AI system itself?

To address this issue, it is essential to establish clear lines of accountability for AI systems. This could involve requiring manufacturers to take responsibility for the actions of their AI systems or establishing regulations that hold AI systems to a certain standard of safety and performance.

Transparency in AI

Finally, *transparency* is another critical ethical consideration in AI. As AI systems become more prevalent in our society, it is essential to ensure that they are transparent and understandable. This means that individuals should be able to understand how AI systems are making decisions and why they are making those decisions. Additionally, AI systems should be auditable, meaning that their decision-making processes can be reviewed and evaluated.

Transparency is particularly important in areas like healthcare and criminal justice, where decisions made by AI systems can have significant consequences. For example, if an AI system is used to make medical diagnoses, patients should be able to understand how the system arrived at its diagnosis and why that diagnosis was made. Similarly, if an AI system is used to make decisions about criminal sentencing, defendants should be able to understand how the system arrived at its decision and why that decision was made.

Ethical considerations in AI are crucial for ensuring that the technology is developed and used in a responsible and beneficial manner. As AI continues to advance and become more integrated into our daily lives, it is essential that we prioritize ethical considerations such as transparency, accountability, fairness, privacy, and safety. By doing so, we can harness the full potential of AI while mitigating any negative consequences. It is important for all stakeholders, including governments, industry leaders, researchers, and the general public, to engage in ongoing discussions and collaboration to establish ethical guidelines and best practices for the development and use of AI. Ultimately, a human-centric approach to AI ethics can help to ensure that AI is aligned with our values and benefits society as a whole.

Index

A
affective computing 29, 47, 48
autoencoders 12, 34, 38
autoregressive models 34, 35, 38

B
ChatGPT 41, 43, 53
computer vision 2, 22, 24
convolutional neural networks 11, 39

D
deep learning 6, 23, 39, 46

F
feedforward neural networks 11, 13

G
generative adversarial networks (GANs) 34, 38
Generative AI 33, 35, 40

L
limited memory 28, 29

long short-term memory networks 12, 13

M
machine learning 4, 11, 23, 41, 52

N
natural language generation (NLG) 17

R
reactive machines 28
recurrent neural networks 11, 13, 39

S
self-aware 29

T
theory of mind 29

V
variational autoencoders (VAEs) 38